I0821244

Additional artwork © Shutterstock 2024 VectorPlotnikoff; fox_workshop; GraphicsRF.com; ActiveLines; SpicyTruffel

Published by Sequoia Kids Media,
an imprint of Sequoia Publishing & Media, LLC

Sequoia Publishing & Media, LLC,
a division of Phoenix International Publications, Inc.

8501 West Higgins Road, Chicago, Illinois 60631
34 Seymour Street, London W1H 7JE
Heimhuder Straße 81, 20148 Hamburg

CustomerService@PhoenixInternational.com

www.PhoenixInternational.com

Library of Congress Control Number: 2024941395

ISBN: 979-8-7654-1000-4

Written by Cassie Gitkin & Kathleen Hanrahan
Illustrated by Gabriele Antonini, Agnieszka Jatkowska,
Tim Warren & Hannah Wood

An imprint of PHOENIX International Publications, Inc.

Being healthy and keeping clean go hand in hand!

The world is full of tiny living things called germs. Some germs are good, but some can make you sick. These tiny things are everywhere: in the air, on the ground, and even on you! Germs, along with dirt and other icky things, stick to the skin on your hands. You don't want those germs and dirt getting into your mouth or onto others.

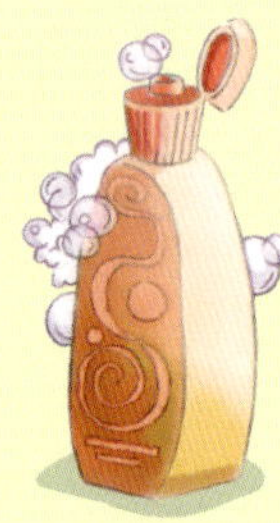

It's important to wash your hands throughout the day to get rid of those yucky things so you and the people around you stay healthy!

When it's time to wash your hands, here's what you do!

Wet: Turn on the water and get your hands wet.

Lather: Add soap to your hands.

Scrub: Rub your hands together. Get between your fingers!

Rinse: Put your hands under the water. Rub until all the soap is gone.

Dry: Use a clean towel to dry your hands.

Now that you know how to wash your hands, it's time to learn when you should do it!

In the Bathroom

After using the potty...

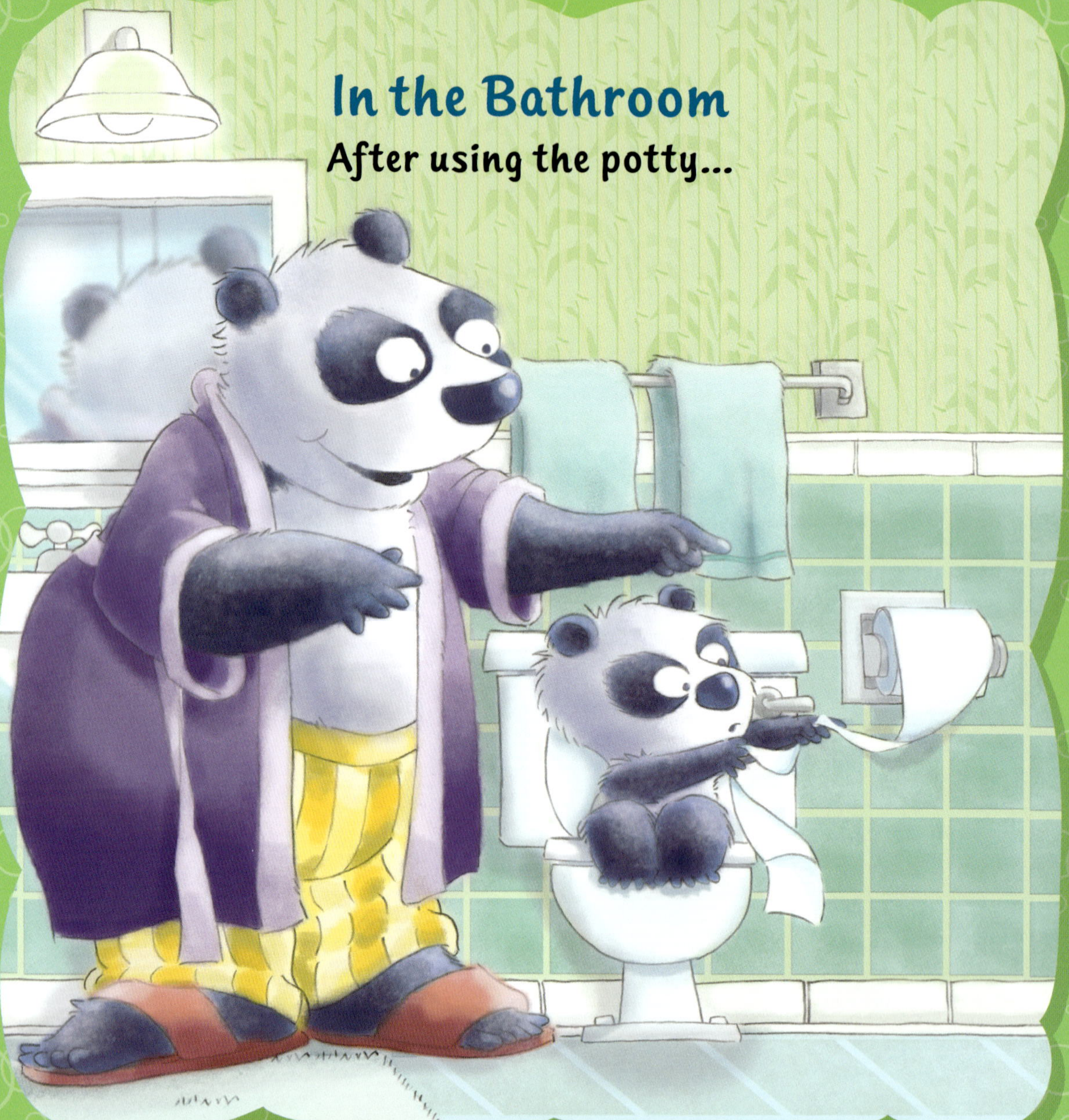

Wash your hands for at least 20 seconds.

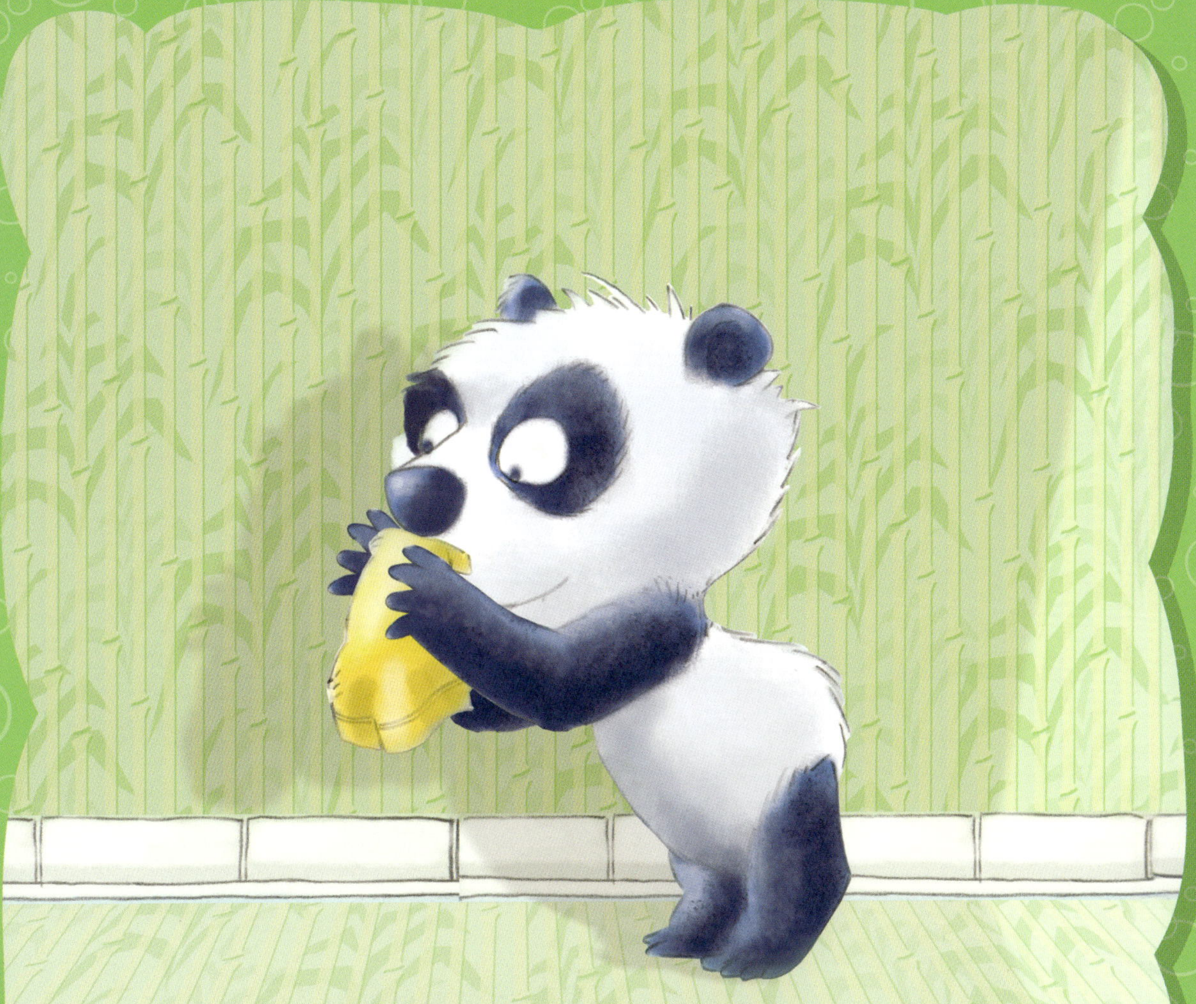

Or blowing your nose...

It's time to wash your hands!

Activity Time

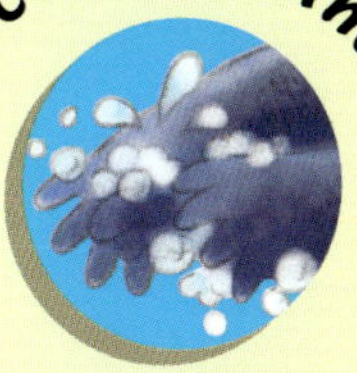

Sing "Twinkle Twinkle Little Star" when you wash your hands. When the song is over, your hands are clean!

At Home

Before you eat...

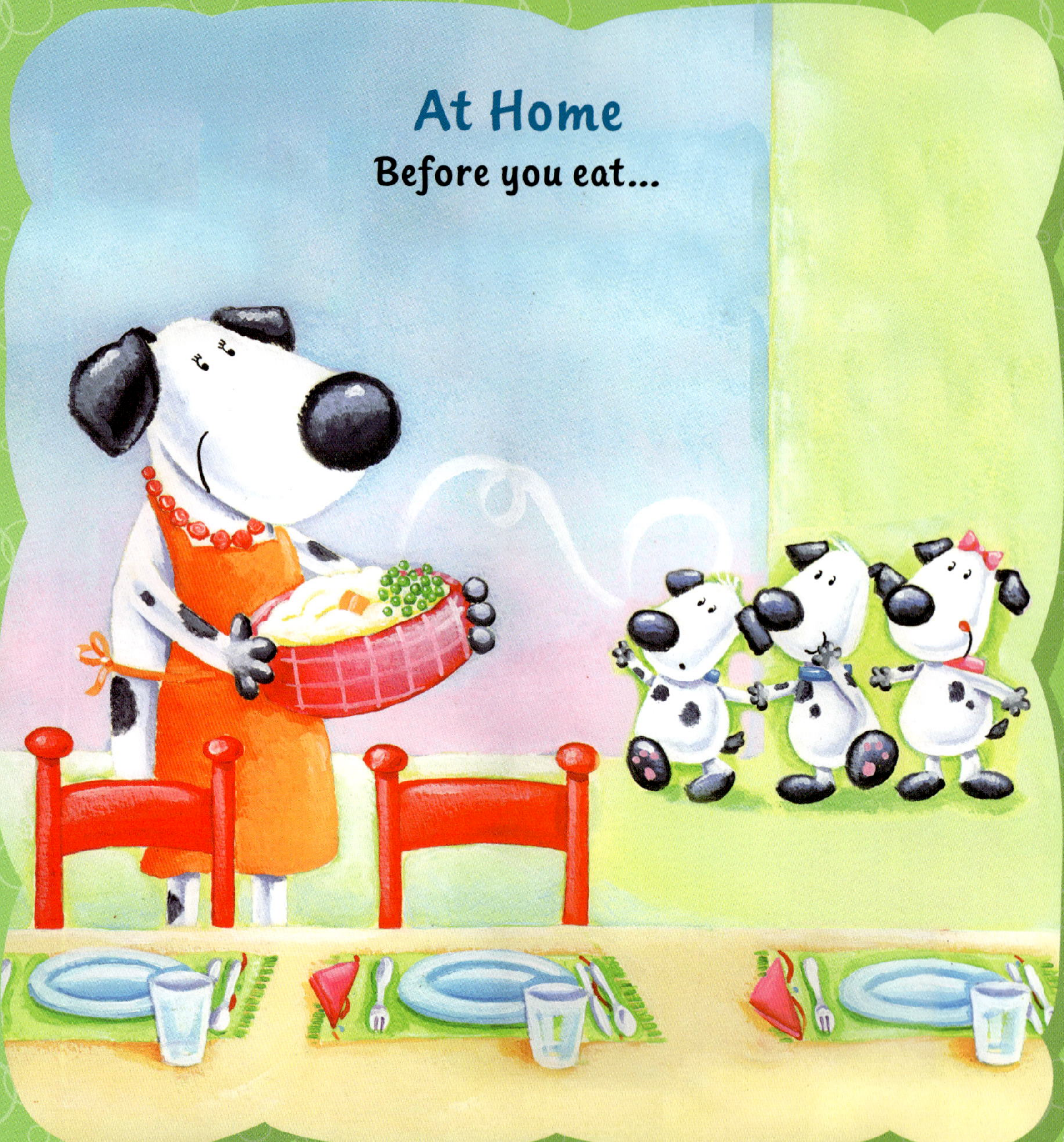

When you can, use warm water to wash your hands.

And after you eat...

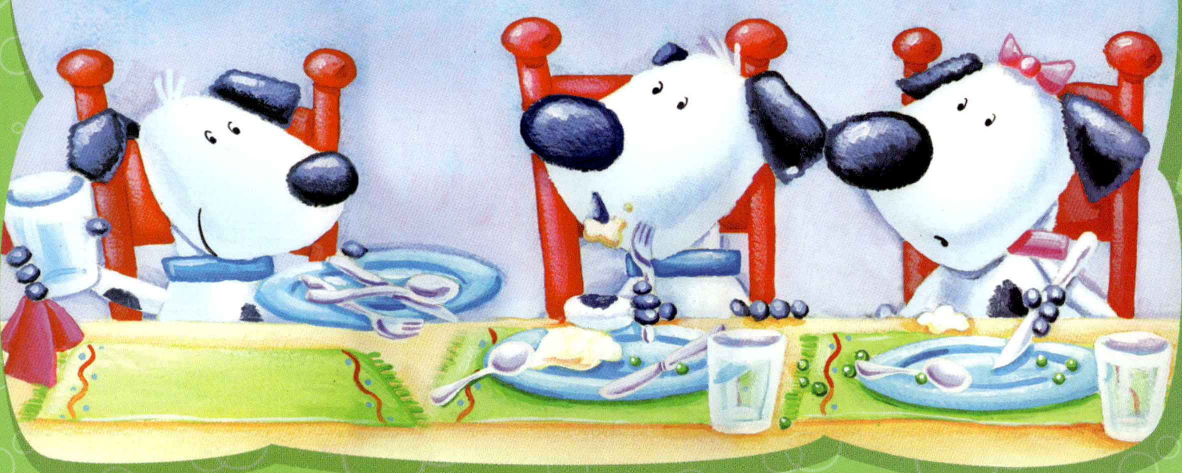

It's time to wash your hands!

Activity Time

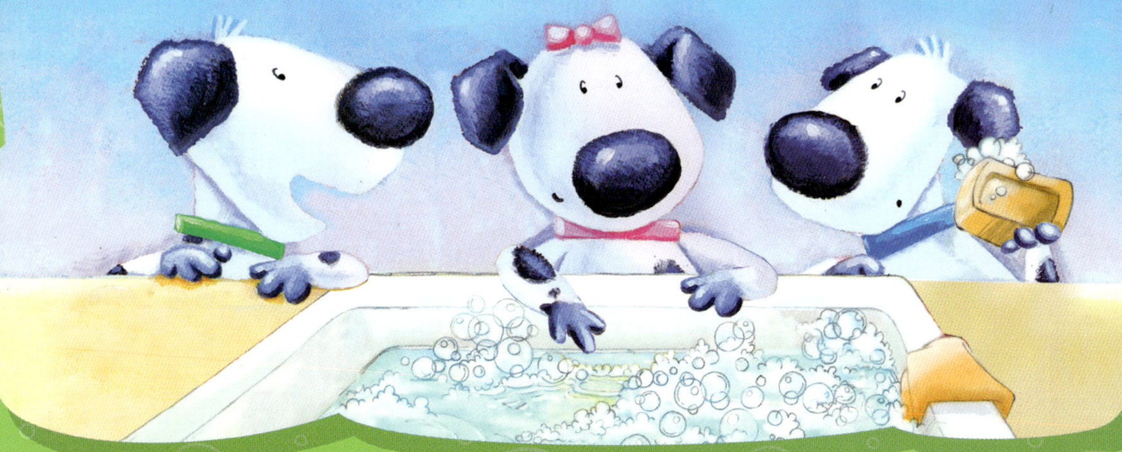

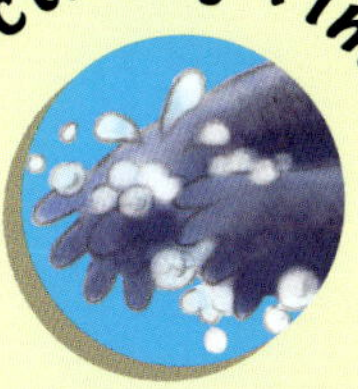

Once your hands are clean after dinner, use your washing skills to help wash the dishes.

At School

After coughing or sneezing...

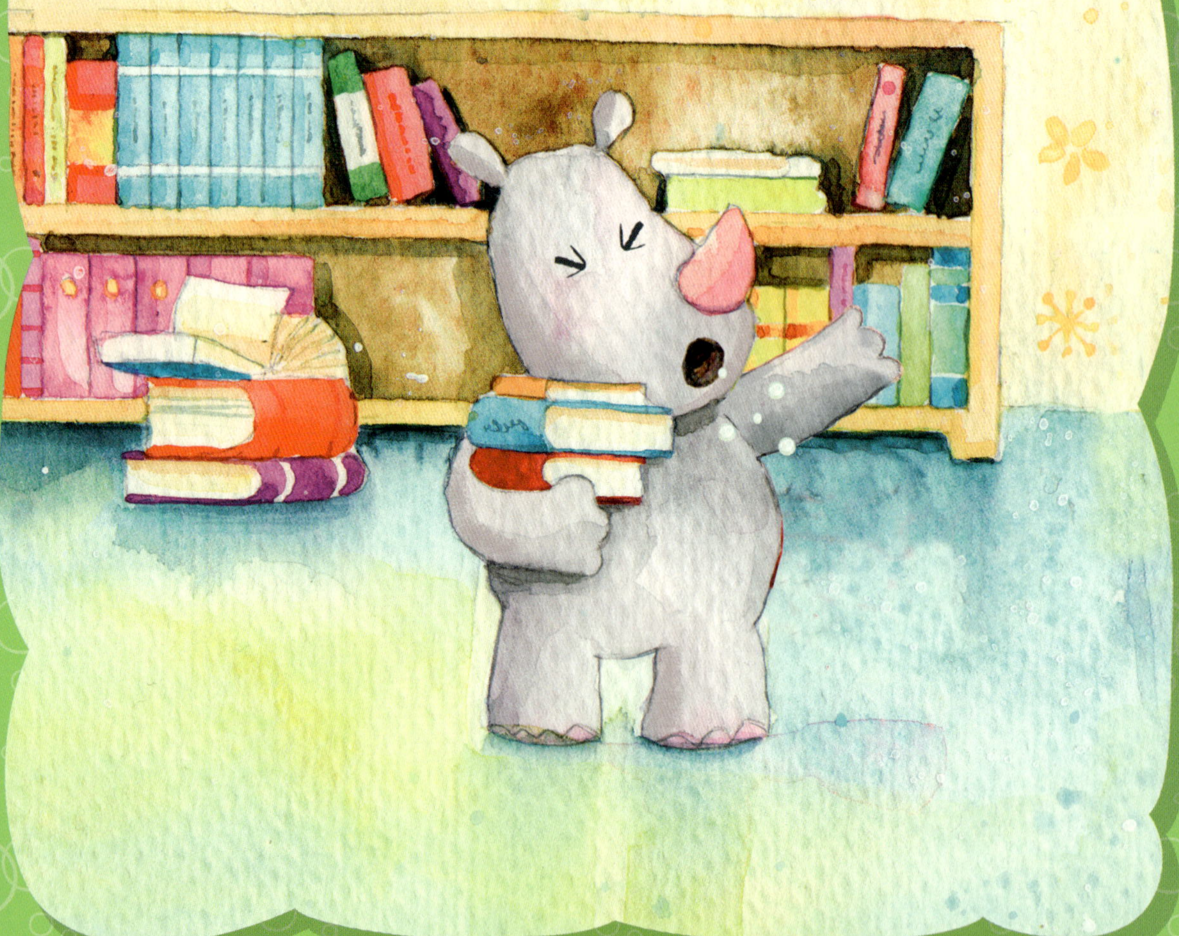

Coughing and sneezing into your elbow keeps your hands clean and helps you avoid spreading germs.

Or holding a pet...

It's time to wash your hands!

Activity Time

Name the three things you use to wash your hands!

At Recess

After playing with friends...

People can't see germs with their eyes alone. The germs are too tiny! Even if your hands look clean, it's a good idea to wash them just in case.

Or if your hands just look dirty...

It´s time to wash your hands!

Activity Time

Put a sticker chart next to the sink.
Add a sticker every time you wash your hands!

At a Birthday Party

Before you eat cake...

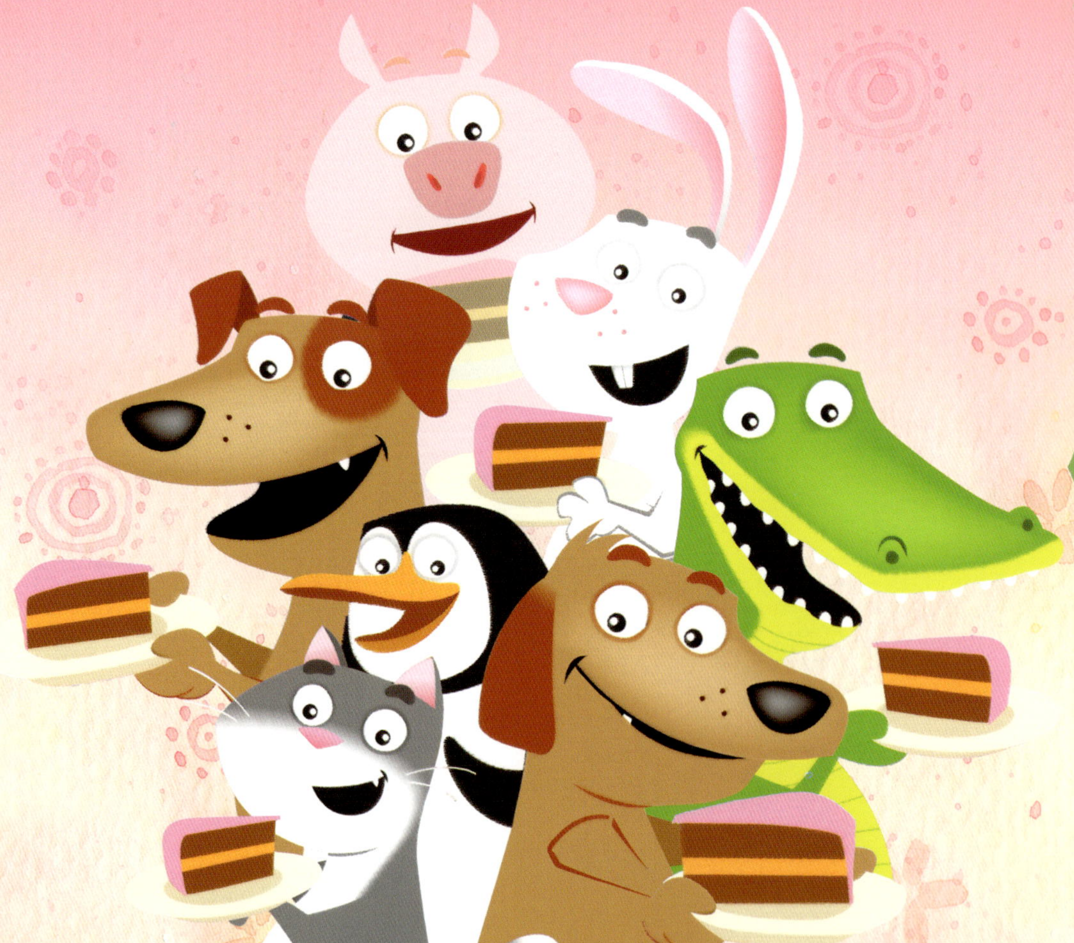

Hygiene Tip

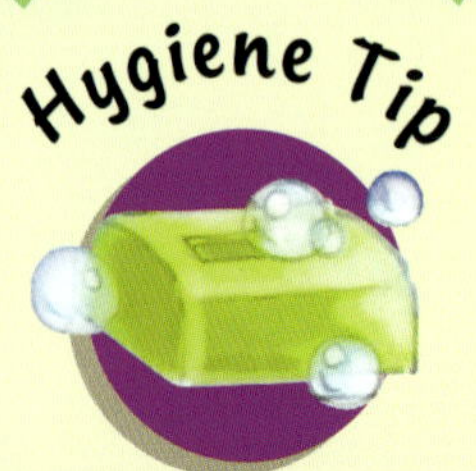

Food that falls on the floor could be covered with germs. When that happens, the safest thing to do is to throw away or compost that food!

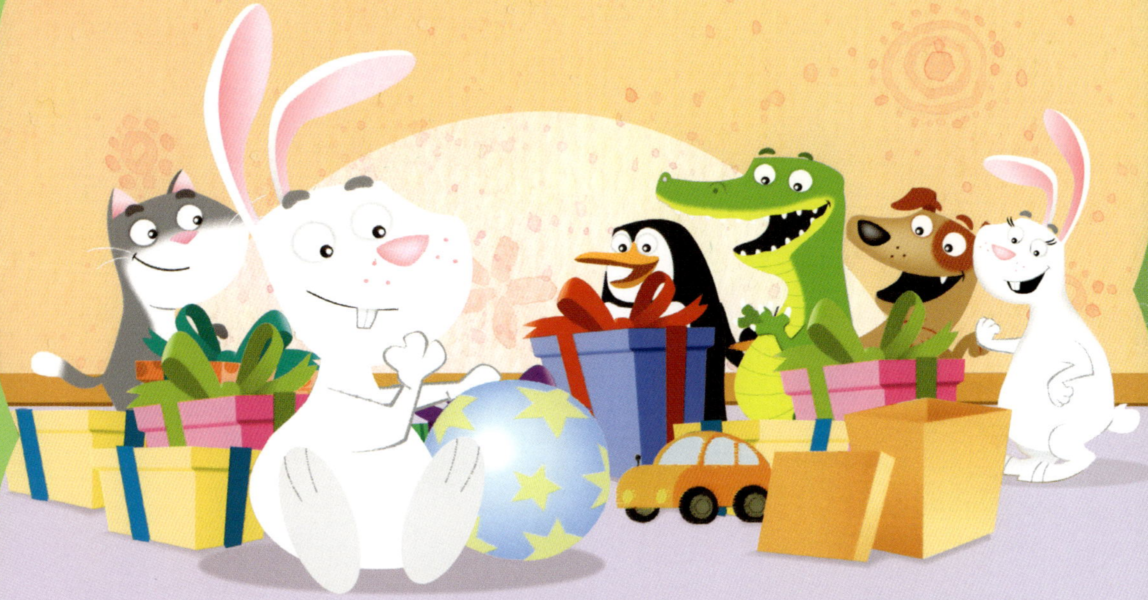

Or after sharing toys...

It's time to wash your hands!

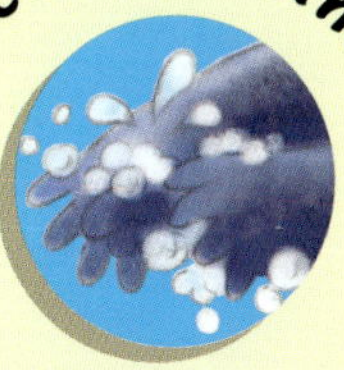

Dolls and action figures get dirty, too!
Wash them clean in the sink.

At the Store

After opening the door...

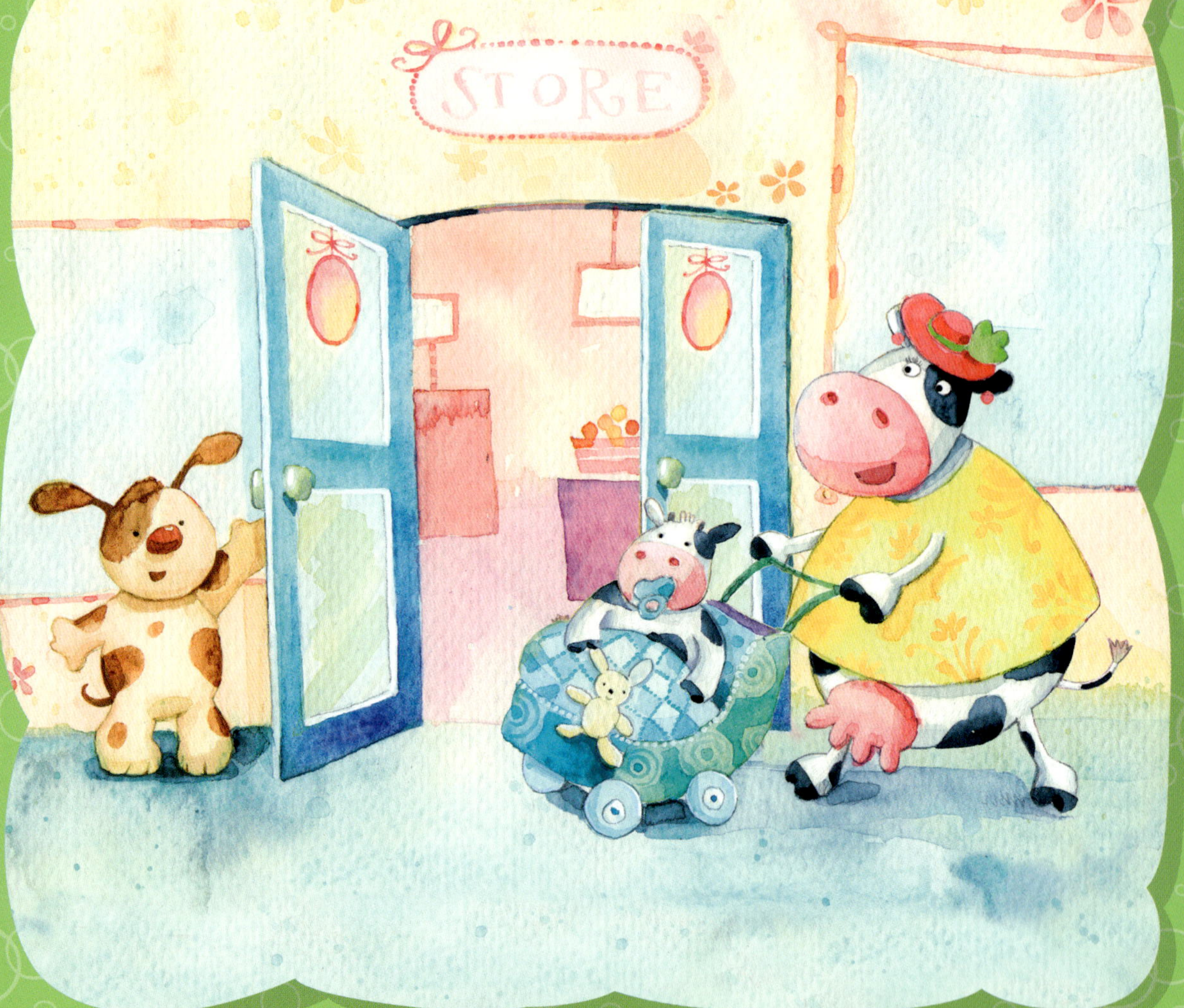

Fruits and vegetables can be covered in icky things, too. Be sure to wash produce from the store before you eat it.

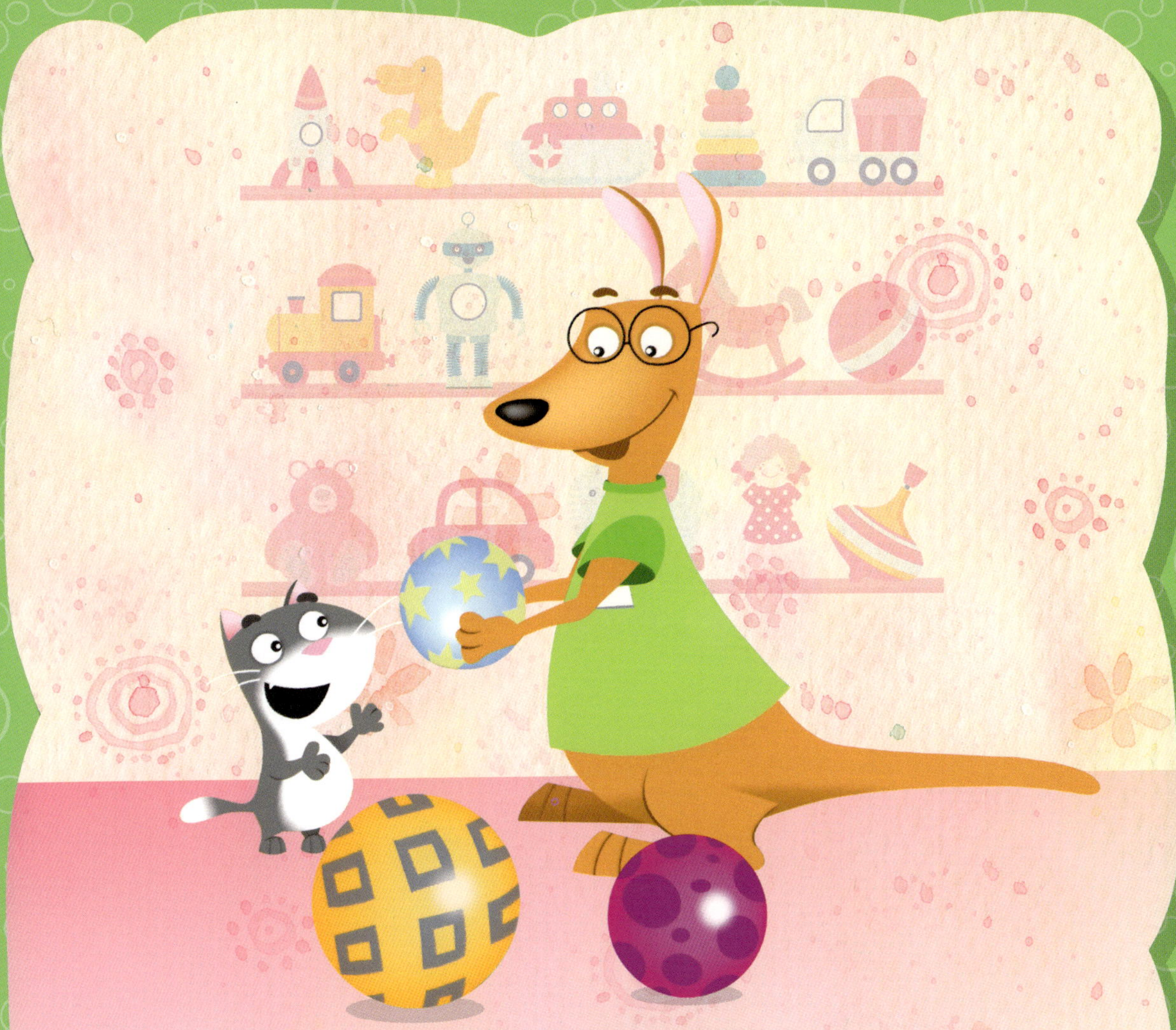

Or buying a new toy...

It´s time to wash your hands!

Activity Time

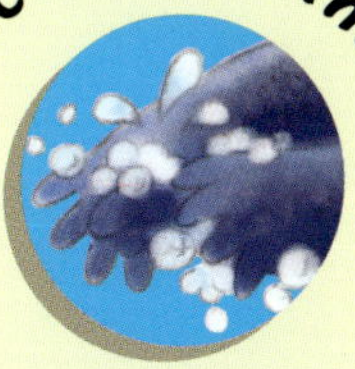

Instead of germs, spread good advice! Help your friends know when and how to wash their hands.

At the Park

After cleaning up...

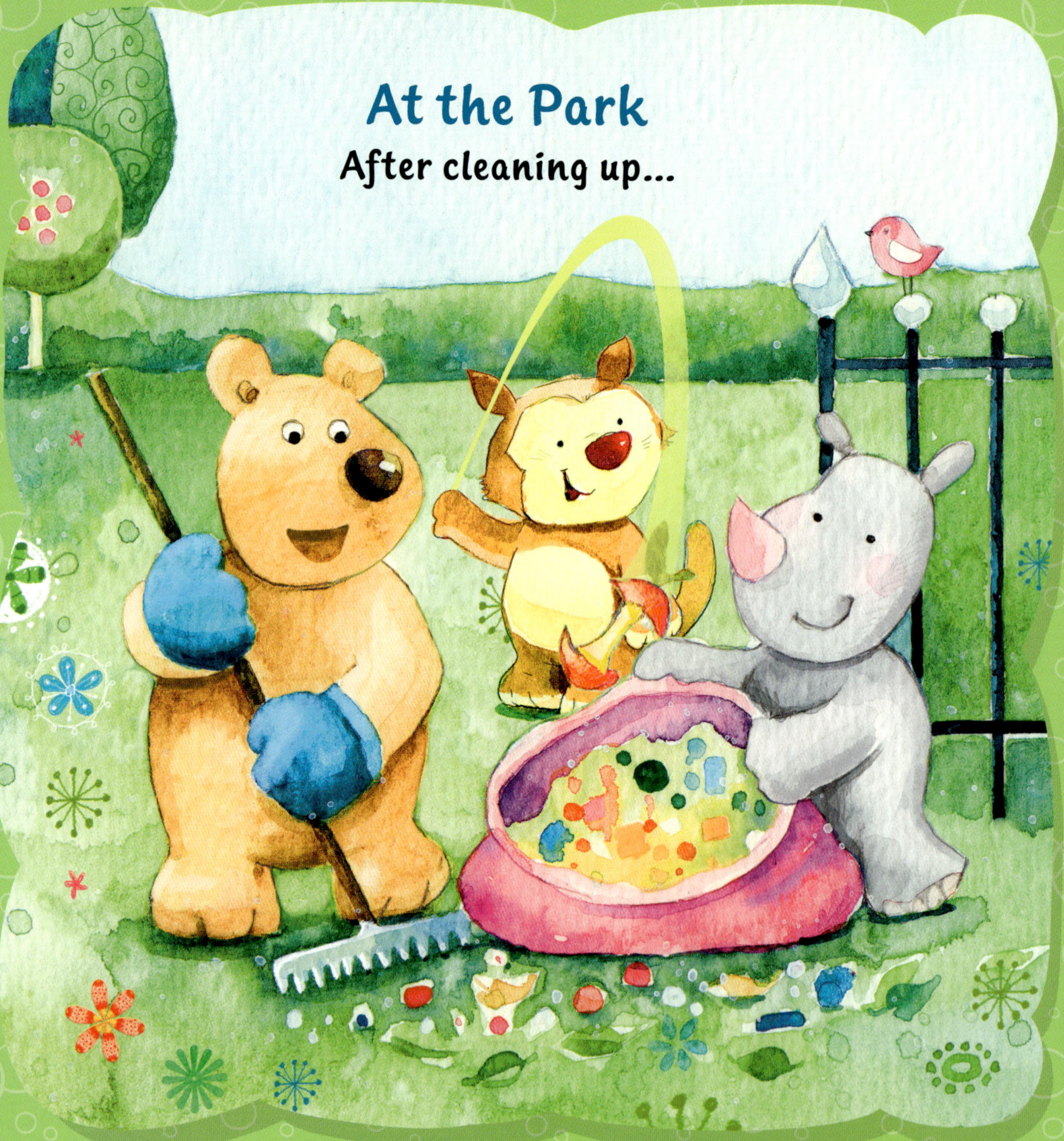

If you aren't near soap and water, you can use hand sanitizer to wash your hands.

Activity Time

A day of playing and sweating can make your whole body dirty. When that happens, it's time to take a bath!